$29.227 Bla
aine, Victor,
bike /
.25

3 4028 09626 5856
HARRIS COUNTY PUBLIC LIBRARY

D0917995

# MY BIKE WITHDRAWN

Victor Blaine

**PowerKiDS** press.

New York

Published in 2015 by The Rosen Publishing Group, Inc.
29 East 21st Street, New York, NY 10010

Copyright © 2015 by The Rosen Publishing Group, Inc.

All rights reserved. No part of this book may be reproduced in any form without permission in writing from the publisher, except by a reviewer.

First Edition

Editor: Sarah Machajewski
Book Design: Mickey Harmon

Photo Credits: Cover, p. 1 spotmatik/Shutterstock.com; p. 5 Jacek Chabraszewski/Shutterstock.com; p. 6 Alinute Silzeviciute/Shutterstock.com; p. 9 KPG_Payless/Shutterstock.com; p. 10 fotum/Shutterstock.com; p. 13 lasalus/Shutterstock.com; p. 14 FXQuadro/Shutterstock.com; p. 17 Paul Vasarhelyi/Shutterstock.com; p. 18 (main) Aleskey Stemmer/Shutterstock.com; p. 18 (inset) pjhpix/Shutterstock.com; p. 21 Anton Gvozdikov/Shutterstock.com; p. 22 Monkey Business Images/Shutterstock.com.

Library of Congress Cataloging-in-Publication Data

Blaine, Victor.
My bike / by Victor Blaine.
p. cm. — (Watch me go!)
Includes index.
ISBN 978-1-4994-0259-9 (pbk.)
ISBN 978-1-4994-0237-7 (6-pack)
ISBN 978-1-4994-0250-6 (library binding)
1. Bicycles — Juvenile literature. 2. Bicycles and bicycling. I. Title.
TL412.B53 2015
629.227—d23

Manufactured in the United States of America

CPSIA Compliance Information: Batch #CW15PK: For Further Information contact Rosen Publishing, New York, New York at 1-800-237-9932

# CONTENTS

Do you have a bike? Bikes are fun to ride.

Bikes have two wheels. There is a wheel in front and a wheel in back.

Bike wheels are also called **tires**.
Tires are filled with air.

Riding a bike is simple. Push the **pedals** with your feet.

The pedals move the **chain**.

The chain moves
the back wheel.

Riding a bike can be hard at first. You can use **training wheels** to help you learn.

Bikes have been around for almost 200 years. There have been many kinds of bikes since the first one was made.

Penny-farthings are one kind of bike. They have a big wheel in front and a small wheel in back.

No matter what kind of bike you ride, always wear a helmet!

Harris County Public Library, Houston, TX

# WORDS TO KNOW

chain

pedal

tires

training wheels

# INDEX

# WEBSITES

Due to the changing nature of Internet links, PowerKids Press has developed an online list of websites related to the subject of this book. This site is updated regularly. Please use this link to access the list: www.powerkidslinks.com/wmg/bike